I0751944

First published in New Zealand 2026 by Sarah Ritchie.

© Copyright 2026 Sarah Ritchie.

The right of Sarah Ritchie to be identified as the author of this work in terms of section 96 of the Copyright Act 1994 is hereby asserted. Text and photographs are entirely the work of the author.

This book is copyright. Except for the purpose of fair review, no part may be stored or transmitted in any form or by any means, electronic or mechanical, including recording or storage in any information retrieval system, without permission in writing from the author. No reproduction may be made, whether by photocopying or by any other means, unless a licence has been obtained from the author.

This book is sold subject to the condition that it shall not, by way of trade or otherwise, be lent, re-sold, hired out, or otherwise circulated without the author's prior consent in any form of binding or cover other than that in which it is published and without a similar condition including this condition being imposed on the subsequent purchaser.

Because of the dynamic nature of the Internet, any web addresses or links contained in this book may have changed since publication and may no longer be valid.

ISBN 978-0-473-78553-6

CONTENTS

wn strength? It can b
saying. When we feel
ntrol over to God. It's
f you, like me, have
you out, you may be
you should continue
God's part. We need
e are letting God do
us, and th
needs. To
wishes.
always
whateve
part i
wish
ulti
3 Let go

BETWEEN THE PAGES

There is something quietly extraordinary about wool.

It begins as a humble, natural fibre – soft, unassuming, and deeply rooted in the land. Yet in the hands of makers, it becomes almost limitless. Walk through any wool or fibre expo and you will see it for yourself: the same raw material transformed again and again. Spun into yarn, woven into cloth, knitted, crocheted, sculpted, and felted. Each maker approaches it differently, yet all are connected by the same starting point. That versatility never ceases to inspire me.

Felting, in particular, carries with it a long and fascinating history. For thousands of years, felt was created as a practical material – used for shelter, clothing, and protection from the elements. It was durable, functional, and essential. Today, while those traditional uses still exist, the craft has evolved in remarkable ways.

With the introduction of the felting needle, we have gained the ability to work with precision and intention, shaping fibre in ways that were once unimaginable. What was once purely functional has opened the door to artistic expression. We are no longer limited to what felt does – we can now explore what it can become. In this book, that exploration takes a small but meaningful form.

Bookmarks sit quietly between the pages of our lives. They hold our place, mark our progress, and often accompany moments of rest, learning, and reflection. Yet they are rarely thought of as art. This collection invites you to see them differently.

Through these projects, you will use wool not just as a material, but as an artistic medium – layering, blending, and shaping fibres to create pieces that are both functional and expressive. Each bookmark becomes a small canvas, a place to experiment, to observe, and to build confidence in your creative decisions.

You don't need to be an artist to begin. You simply need curiosity.

So take your time. Explore the fibre. Notice how it behaves, how colours interact, how texture emerges. Allow yourself to play, to learn, and to create without pressure.

And perhaps, as you work through these pieces, you'll begin to see wool – and your own creativity – in a whole new way.

Sarah Ritchie

WHAT EQUIPMENT WILL YOU NEED?

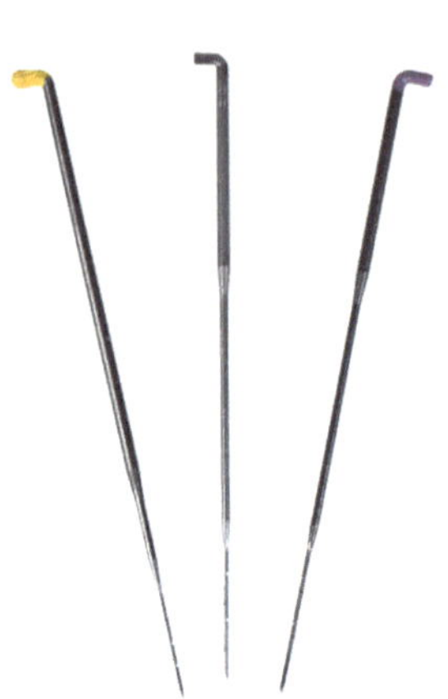

FELTING NEEDLES

QUANTITY

You only need one felting needle to complete any of the projects in this book. However, it's almost guaranteed that you will break at least one needle per project – especially in the early stages of learning to felt, or if you are using poor-quality needles. Good-quality needles cost more but are less prone to breaking. Therefore, in my opinion, it is worth investing in good tools right from the start, as this will make your felting experience far more enjoyable. I recommend purchasing at least four needles to start with. You will want to have a number of spares in your toolbox, should you continue needle-felting in the future.

BRAND

I have experimented with countless needles from multiple suppliers and ultimately settled on the internationally recognised WIZPICK range of colour-coded needles. If you choose to use WIZPICK needles, I recommend purchasing a set, especially if you are serious about continuing with needle-felting (whether 2D or 3D). Keeping this set intact will allow you to use it as a reference guide when selecting the best needle(s) for any given project. Ideally, your master set would include: Lime, Green, Pink, Red, Mauve, Peach, Burgundy, Brown, Cream, Yellow, Gold, Orange, White, Grey, Blue, and Aqua.

From the WIZPICK range, I chose needles based on what worked best with the texture, thickness, and weave of my preferred fabric base, the fibre, and my felting style. My favourite needles are:

- Mauve: 3.5" long, 36-gauge (2x2x2 barbs).
- Peach: 3" long, 38-gauge (2x2x2x2 barbs).
- Yellow: 3.5" long, 40-gauge (2x2x2 barbs).

If you're looking for a general, all-purpose needle for needle-felted painting, I suggest a 36-gauge needle. A good-quality 36-gauge needle can be purchased from suppliers like Ashford Wheels and Looms (ashford-craftshop.co.nz).

Beware of cheap needles! You'll know if you're using a poor-quality needle – it won't feel right. You'll poke the fibre repeatedly, and it will fail to catch properly, or it will take much longer to felt the fibre compared to a good-quality needle. Additionally, poor-quality needles are more likely to break. It's worth investing in high-quality needles early on so that you can quickly learn what "good" vs "poor" quality feels like.

LENGTH

You may prefer a 3" length, or the longer 3.5" length – the feel as you hold and use the needle is slightly different for each. It is also important to remember that electric felting tools, or handles that hold multiple needles may suit or require one length over the other.

TYPE

In addition to gauge, length, and barb configuration, you will encounter the following types of needles available for purchase:

- Triangle (a.k.a. Regular): For all-purpose 2D or 3D felting and 3D shaping. This is the type you should use for the needle-felted projects in this book.
- Star: For faster felting of larger areas or firming. While star needles are effective for some felters, I've found no noticeable difference for the type of fibre projects shown in this book.
- Spiral: For smoother finishes with fewer needle marks. Since you'll be ironing your work at the end of the fibre painting process, needle marks will not be an issue for you.
- Reverse: For creating textures and fluffing fur or hair effects. The barbs face the opposite direction, pulling fibres out rather than pushing them in. You may choose to use this effect in your fibre art, however reverse needles are not used to create the projects in this book.
- Crown (a.k.a. Ultra): For precision and fine detail work, predominantly used for 3D projects.
- Fork: For gentle blending and surface work, often used in doll-making.

NEEDLE HANDLE

Felting without a handle involves pinching the needle tightly between your forefinger and thumb, which can lead to strain or discomfort in your fingers, hand, or wrist – especially during long felting sessions. A needle handle helps to reduce this strain by providing a more comfortable grip, making the process easier on your hands.

There are many handle styles available, ranging from simple and inexpensive wooden holders to ergonomically designed handles. Some handles are designed to hold a single needle, while others can hold multiple needles at once.

Single-needle handles offer the greatest degree of precision and control, making them ideal for detailed work.

Multi-needle handles are excellent for covering large areas quickly, as they allow you to work with several needles at once, reducing the time and effort needed for felting larger sections.

It's worth having both types of handles in your toolbox so you can switch between them depending on the task at hand.

Ultimately, the handle you choose should feel comfortable in your hand and suit your style of felting. Experiment with a few options to find the ones that work best for you.

My personal preferences are a simple wooden single-needle handle from Temu (#3, below) and a Clover 3-needle handle (#2, below). It's worth noting that while you can purchase an identical 3-needle handle from Temu, the needles provided are of poor quality. You might consider purchasing the more affordable handle then replace the needles with your preferred high quality needles for the best results.

FOAM BASE

When it comes to the substrate you felt into, felters have their own unique preferences and ways of working. Common bases include:

- Foam: The most widely used base for needle-felting and the base used for the projects in this book.

NEEDLE HANDLES

1 Example of a multi-needle tool.
2 Clover Pen Style Needle Felting Tool (multi-needle), clover-usa.com.
3 Simple single-needle holder, available from websites such as Temu.
4 Handle for those with grip issues, available from marieraddingarts.com (search "needle felting handle").
5 Example of an electric needle-felting tool (not recommended for projects in this book).

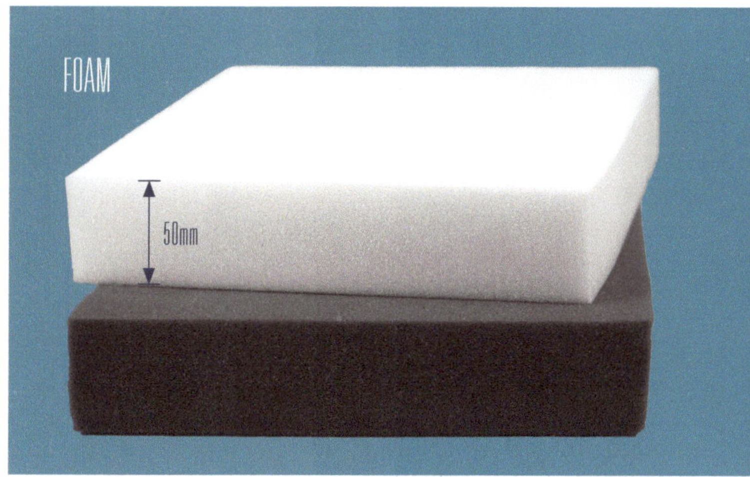

FOAM

- Cotton canvas: Similar to what you would use for painting, stretched over a frame.
- Embroidery hoops: Ideal for smaller projects, as they hold the fabric taut.
- Tapestry frames: Sometimes useful for larger works to keep the fabric stretched and stable.

My personal preference is to use 50mm thick, high-density foam (commonly used in upholstery), cut to the same size or slightly larger than your fabric. I secure the fabric to the foam with pins to ensure the fabric stays in place during the felting process.

The 50mm depth is essential because it provides enough cushioning to prevent your needle from reaching the bottom and scratching your table or easel. Additionally, it helps to protect the needle from becoming dull or breaking, which can happen if it repeatedly hits a hard surface beneath a thinner foam base.

Of all the pieces of needle-felting equipment, the foam base is likely to be one of the more expensive investments. However, it's worth selecting good-quality, high-density foam, as cheaper alternatives can disintegrate or lose their integrity after a few uses. A durable foam base will save you time and frustration in the long run, making it a worthwhile addition to your felting toolkit.

BASE FABRIC

For needle-felting you can use almost all natural fabrics (linen, cotton, jute, denim, calico, wool felt sheets, etc.). However, some fabrics work better than others.

Fabric comes in various weights (GSM – grams per square metre) and thread counts (TPI – threads per inch), which determine the coarseness or fineness of the fabric.

For fibre painting, you don't want the threads to be too close together (making it difficult to push the needle through), nor do you want them too far apart (leaving little for the wool fibre to felt into).

When I began needle-felting, I experimented with a wide range of cottons, calicos (unbleached/undyed cotton), and linens to find one that suited my style of felting. I eventually discovered a cotton/linen blend that worked well, although either 100% cotton or 100% linen would also be suitable, provided the TPI and GSM are appropriate.

My advice is this: when you find a fabric that you like, purchase at least a couple of metres, as it might not be available again in the future. It's also worth keeping an eye out for sales, as natural fibre fabrics can be pricey.

To easily transfer the patterns featured in this book, it is best to use a white fabric that is not too dense.

To achieve the fringe effect shown on these bookmarks you will use a top layer of white fabric and a bottom layer of 100% wool felted sheet (see page 9), but you can make a bookmark out of many different materials, with or without the fringe.

Left: 100% wool felt sheet
Right: Cotton/Linen blend fabric

PINS

You'll need a few standard sewing pins to attach the perimeter of fabric and/or felt to the foam base.

EASEL

The easiest and most affordable way to needle-felt the bookmark projects in this book is to work on a flat surface, such as a table. However, spending long periods bent over your work can strain your neck, shoulders, and back.

When I first started needle-felting, I purchased a commercially made tabletop easel, which helped improve my posture by allowing me to adjust the angle of my work. However, due to the downward force involved in needle-felting, I found that the easel tended to tip backwards. To stabilise it, I screwed the base of the easel to a sheet of plywood and added a sandbag to keep it from sliding around.

As my fibre paintings grew larger and no longer fit on the small tabletop easel, I constructed a heavy-duty easel out of plywood. This larger easel features an adjustable base that allows me to raise the artwork to various heights. It has been perfect for all my fibre-painting projects.

Recognising that not everyone has the tools or skills to build a large easel, I've designed a smaller version (see photo page 6) specifically for needle-felting small projects similar to those featured in this book. To purchase the simple pattern and instructions for constructing this easel, visit the shop on my website: sarah-ritchie.com.

PATTERN TRANSFER

Additional equipment you will need for transferring the pattern to the fabric:

- A fine black permanent marker or black ballpoint pen.
- Masking tape (a.k.a. 'painter's tape') or other tape.
- A ruler or straight edge.
- A lightbox or lightpad (or you can use a window!).

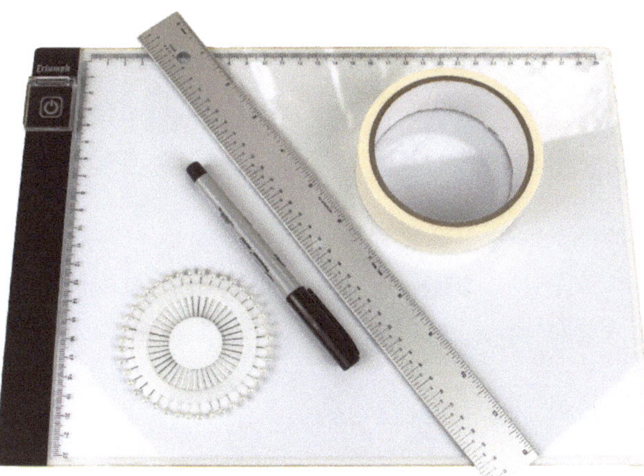

CARDING BRUSHES

To prepare and blend the fibre for all the projects in this book, you can simply use your fingers. However, if you wish to speed up the process or create a blend where the fibres are well-mixed, you may want to use carding brushes.

There are many different brands and sizes of carding brushes available, although they can be quite pricey. I have found that good-quality, second-hand carding brushes work well, as they were built to last.

For the small amounts of fibre used in these projects, you'll only need two small carding brushes or drum carder cleaning brushes. Alternatively, you could use two wire-bristle dog brushes, though keep in mind that the wire bristles may weaken and become ineffective over time, as they are not specifically designed for fibre carding.

Pictured: An old Tekoteko hand carder (left) – if you can find one of these second-hand, buy it, they are amazing! An Ashford Flick Carder (right) from ashfordcraftshop.co.nz.

FIBRE

WHAT TYPE OF FIBRE SHOULD YOU USE?

That's a great question, and one with a slightly complex answer, as fibre can vary from country to country. When it comes to wool, each country has its own breeds of sheep, and even wool from the same breed can feel different depending on factors like climate, diet, and farming practices.

Some sheep breeds are particularly well suited for needle-felting – Corriedale and Merino are popular choices known for their ability to felt well and blend smoothly.

On the other hand, some breeds don't felt well at all and may cause frustration, especially if the fibre is coarse, hairy, or lacks sufficient 'crimp' (the natural waviness that helps fibres bind together). Breeds in this category include Cheviot, Dorset, Romney, Lincoln, Suffolk, and Karakul.

Some other natural fibres can also be challenging. Angora, Mohair, Llama, and Alpaca are difficult to needle-felt because they are smooth and lack the scale structure of wool. While Alpaca is wonderful for wet-felting, it can be too slippery for effective needle-felting.

One useful guide is the micron count of the fibre. Higher micron wool (e.g. Romney: 35–40 microns, Lincoln: 38–45 microns) is coarser and better suited to robust projects. For fibre painting, where a smooth finish is desired, Corriedale (25–30 microns) or Merino (18–24 microns) is ideal. Generally, the lower the micron count, the finer and softer the wool. For beginners, I recommend starting with Corriedale or Merino.

If you have access to a local fibre suppliers, it's worth experimenting to find what works best for you.

USING COTTON FIBRE FOR HIGHLIGHTS

In addition to wool fibre, the patterns in this book use small amounts of white cotton fibre to create bright highlights.

White wool fibre is often off-white, whereas cotton fibre gives a much cleaner, brighter white. This contrast is important for creating definition between highlights and shadows in your work.

Cotton fibre should be used sparingly, and only on Layer 4. It is a denser fibre, and using it in earlier layers increases the risk of breaking your needle.

To help it felt into your work, combine a small amount of cotton fibre with a little wool fibre (either white or coloured). This will help it bind more effectively to the layers beneath.

WHAT COLOUR FIBRES DO YOU NEED?

You'll notice that the patterns in this book use a range of colours. However, you are free to choose your own palette from the fibres you already have. Your finished bookmarks will look different from mine, and that's absolutely fine.

When starting out, it's easy to feel overwhelmed by colour choices. The good news is that you don't need every colour.

Fibres can be blended to create the illusion of new colours (see page 11). Rather than physically mixing fibres, you are blending visually – similar to the technique used by Pointillist painters.

To begin, you only need a few core fibres: the primary colours (red, blue, yellow), plus black and white (both white wool fibre and white cotton fibre for highlights). These will allow you to create a wide range of tones (see photo below).

You can darken a colour by adding black, or lighten it by adding white.

Adding secondary colours to your supply (orange, green, and purple) will increase your colour palette and make blending even easier.

Of course, if you get hooked on needle-felting, then there is a world of colour fibre that awaits you!

HOW MUCH FIBRE DO YOU NEED?

The patterns in this book require only small amounts of fibre, making this a great way to use up your scraps.

Fibre is often sold in 100g (3.5oz) packs per colour, so you will have much more than you need for these projects. If you are just starting out, purchasing sample packs is a great option. This allows you to build a range of colours in smaller quantities – perfect for bookmarks.

My fibre of preference is the Ashford Corriedale range, as it needle-felts exceptionally well and offers consistent colours that can be repurchased over time. Ashford fibre (single colours, theme packs, and sample packs) is available online at ashfordcraftshop.co.nz.

Remember, you can also use the fibres and colours available in your local area.

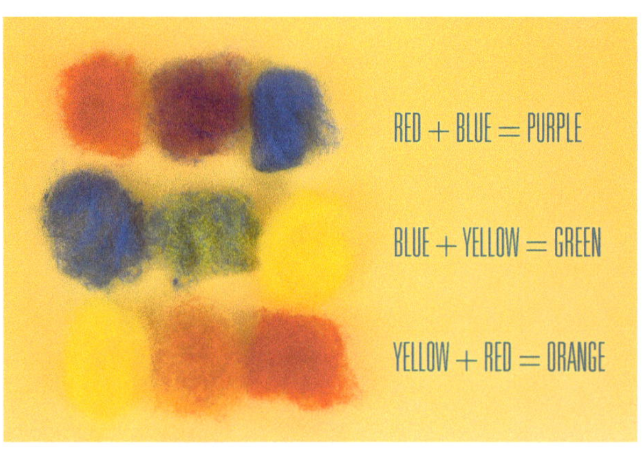

MATERIAL FOR THE FRINGE EFFECT

The fringing shown in this book is just one way of finishing your bookmark (see page 25 for more finishing ideas).

If you would like to create a fringe effect, you will need to use **two layers of material**.

The top layer is a white fabric (I used a cotton–linen blend). This is the layer you will transfer your pattern onto. The fringe is created by the horizontal and vertical threads in the weave of the fabric.

The bottom layer is a 100% wool felt sheet. This provides rigidity to the bookmark and support for the fringing. You can create a fringe without this felt layer, however the bookmark will be quite floppy.

If using a wool felt backing, it is important that you use **100% wool** felt, rather than a synthetic alternative (commonly found in craft stores), for two key reasons:

1 You need a natural fibre base for the wool fibres to needle-felt into and bind with.

2 Needle-felting into a synthetic base is much harder on your hands, and your fingers and wrist are likely to become sore quite quickly.

If you can only source a synthetic felt sheet, it is better to use it as a backing layer and glue it to the top fabric at the end of the process, rather than needle-felt into it.

As you transfer your pattern, take a moment to **line up the edges of the bookmark with the horizontal and vertical threads in the fabric**. This small step makes a big difference, ensuring your fringe sits neatly and parallel to the edges.

BEWARE – NOT ALL WOOL FELT SHEETS ARE CREATED EQUAL

Wool felt can be purchased in a wide range of sizes and made from different types of wool fibre. It is available by the sheet or by the metre, and can vary from very soft to quite firm. For our purposes, you are ideally looking for a medium-density wool felt.

The image (right) shows the same pattern ('Whisker', page 56) needle-felted onto two different felt densities. Sample (A) was created using very soft felt on the bottom layer, while (B) uses a medium-density felt.

You can see that (B) has much greater definition, with sharper lines and cleaner colours. You may also notice that (A) has stretched slightly out of shape.

100% wool felt sheets are not always easy to find, so sometimes it is a case of using what is available. However, if you have access to a few options, it is well worth doing a small test first to see which felt gives you the best result.

FOR YOUR SAFETY

While needle-felting is a relaxing and creative craft, it's important to prioritise safety to avoid injuries and discomfort. The sharp needles and repetitive motions involved in this art form require proper handling and workspace setup. By following these tips, you can ensure a safer and more enjoyable needle-felting experience.

HANDLING NEEDLES SAFELY

- Always handle your needle with care to avoid accidental injury.
- Keep your fingers clear of the needle's path as you work.
- Insert the needle straight in and pull it straight out; avoid bending or twisting the needle to prevent breakage.
- Protect your fingers, especially when working on smaller areas or with tiny bits of fibre. Some felters use finger guards (below), though I prefer to be able to feel the fibre for greater control.
- Store needles safely when not in use and keep them out of the reach of children and animals.

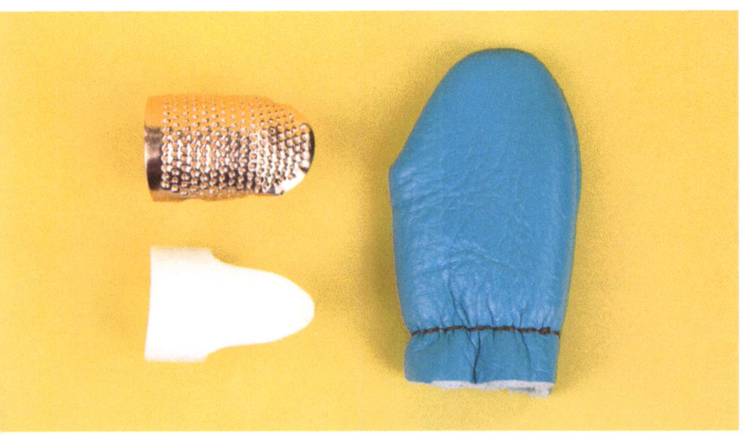

LOOKING AFTER YOUR BODY

- Use a comfortable chair or stool that allows you to maintain good posture while working.
- Sit upright with your back straight and shoulders relaxed.
- Needle-felting involves repetitive movements; take regular breaks to rest your hands and wrists and avoid strain or injury.
- Stretch your fingers, hands, and wrists frequently to maintain flexibility and reduce the risk of repetitive strain injuries (RSI).
- Use a needle handle to make needle-felting more comfortable and reduce hand strain.
- Work in a well-lit area to minimise eye strain and ensure you can see your work clearly.
- Use a desk lamp or position your workspace near natural light for optimal visibility.

DISPOSING OF BROKEN NEEDLES

Even the most careful needle-felter will break many needles – it's part of the process. For each fibre painting, expect one or two breakages.

When a needle breaks, ensure you locate the broken tip. It's essential to remove it from your artwork or retrieve it from where it has fallen.

Store broken needles (both shafts and tips) in a secure container – a small disposable container works well. Once full, tape it closed and dispose of it carefully to ensure safety.

By following these safety tips, you can enjoy your needle-felting projects with peace of mind, reducing the risk of injury and discomfort.

COLOUR THEORY

Unlike painting, where you can mix colours directly, needle-felting requires you to *blend* fibres to create the illusion of different colours. I call that "tricking the eye". This makes understanding colour theory even more important, as it helps you achieve the desired effects by combining fibres effectively.

Have you ever wondered why some colour combinations sing whilst others clash or look muddy? That's colour theory in action. If you follow these tried and tested colour rules, you can't go wrong and you'll end up with artwork that looks delicious!

You can use the colour wheel (pictured right), to assist you to make colour choices that work well together. You can also use the colour wheel to determine the colours that you'll need to blend together to create the resulting colour that you want.

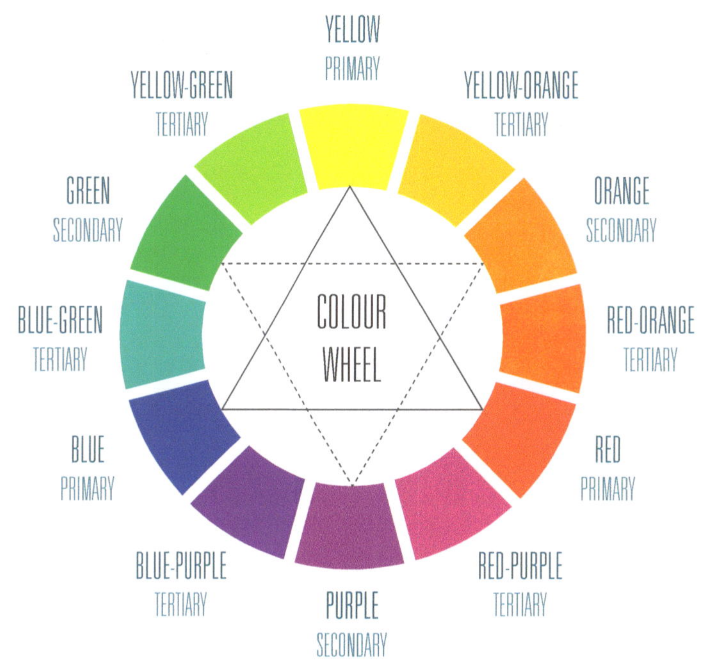

PRIMARY COLOURS

The primary colours are red, blue, and yellow. These colours cannot be created by mixing other colours. They serve as the base for creating all other colours.

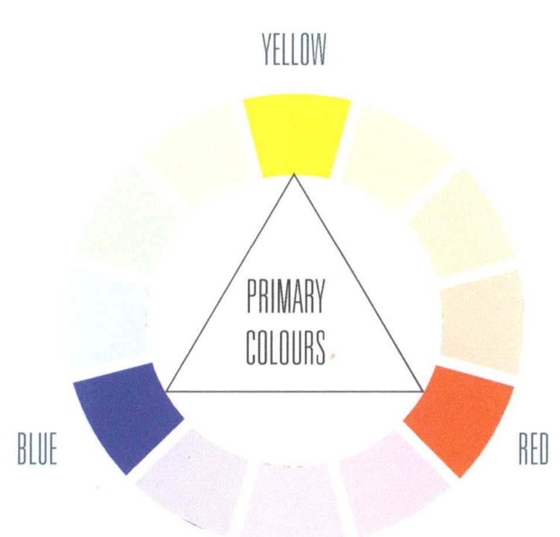

SECONDARY COLOURS

Secondary colours are green, orange, and purple (a.k.a. violet). These are created by blending two primary colours:

Red + Blue = Purple (Violet)

Blue + Yellow = Green

Yellow + Red = Orange

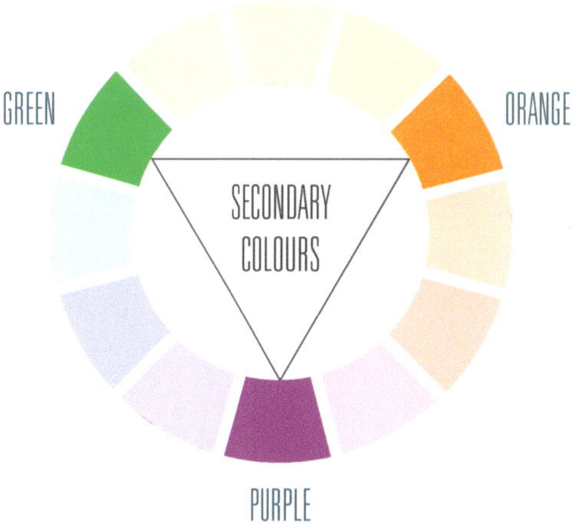

TERTIARY COLOURS

Tertiary colours are created by blending a primary colour with a secondary colour:

Red + Orange = Red-Orange
Yellow + Orange = Yellow-Orange
Yellow + Green = Yellow-Green
Blue + Green = Blue-Green
Blue + Purple = Blue-Purple (a.k.a. Blue-Violet)
Red + Purple = Red-Purple (a.k.a. Red-Violet)

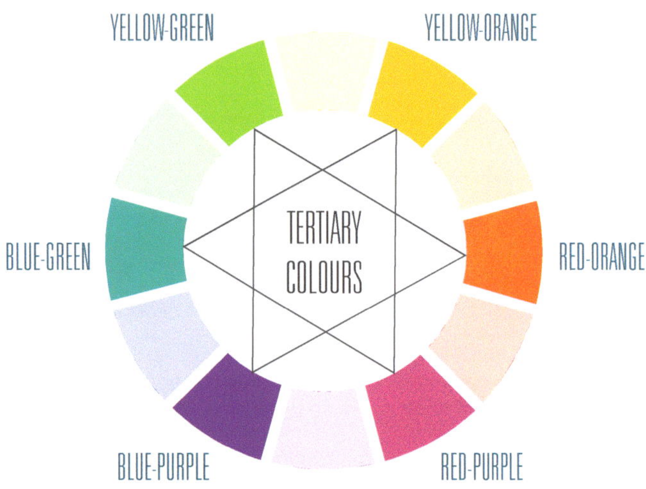

COMPLEMENTARY COLOURS

Complementary colours are opposite each other on the colour wheel (e.g. red and green, blue and orange, yellow and purple). When shown next to each other in a fibre painting, they create strong contrast and can make each other appear more vibrant.

ANALOGOUS COLOURS

Analogous colours are next to each other on the colour wheel (e.g. yellow, yellow-green, and green). These colours often work well when shown together in a fibre painting, and create serene and comfortable designs.

ADJUSTING WARMTH OR COOLNESS

Add a touch of yellow to warm up a colour, or blue to cool it down. For example, adding yellow to green creates a warmer lime green, while adding blue to green creates a cooler teal.

SOFTENING COLOURS

Add a small amount of a complementary colour to soften a bright or saturated colour. For example, adding a touch of blue to orange can create a subtle, burnt-orange shade.

CREATING SHADES AND TINTS

You won't always want to use bright, pure primary, secondary and tertiary colours. You might wish to create darker or lighter versions of these colours, which are known as 'shades' and 'tints'. This can help you create more dimension and interest in your artwork.

When mixing shades or tints, avoid adding both black and white to the same colour simultaneously, as this can create a dull, muddy effect.

To create **shades**, blend a colour with varying amounts of black (this example uses yellow as the base colour). Be cautious, as black can overpower the original colour quickly.

To create **tints**, blend a colour with varying amounts of white (this example uses yellow as the base colour).

To create pink, add white to red.

BROWN

It's easy to accidentally make brown by blending random fibres together. It's more skilful to create the type of brown that you want by getting your blends right according to colour theory.

To create brown from primary and secondary coloured fibres, you need to mix *complementary* colours in roughly equal amounts (colours that are opposite each other on the colour wheel). Here's how you can do it:

Orange + Blue. Adjust the ratio to make the brown warmer (more orange) or cooler (more blue).

Green + Red. Add slightly more red to create a warmer brown or more green for an earthier tone.

Purple + Yellow. For a lighter brown, add more yellow. For a richer, darker brown, increase the amount of purple.

TRANSFERRING YOUR PATTERN

The first step is to photocopy or scan your chosen pattern from this book. Use standard 80gsm (or thinner) white paper so that light can easily pass through it. Choose the transfer method that best suits your base material, and leave enough fabric around the edge of the design to allow you to pin your work to the foam base.

LIGHT-BASED TRANSFER

If your fabric is light in colour and slightly transparent, you can transfer the pattern using a light source.

Place your pattern beneath your fabric and use either a light pad/light box or tape both layers to a window. This will allow you to see the pattern lines clearly through the fabric.

Trace the image onto your fabric using a permanent marker or black ballpoint pen. The lines do not need to be perfect – any small inaccuracies will be covered by fibre as you work.

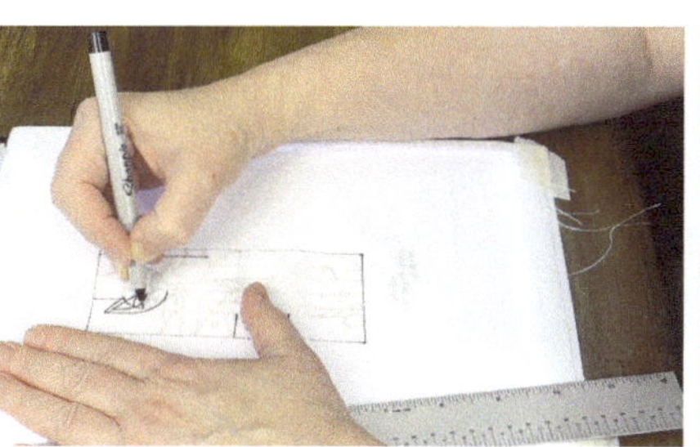

TRANSFER PAPER OR INTERFACING

If your fabric is too opaque or dark to see through, you can use either water-soluble stabiliser or fusible interfacing.

Both of these act as a temporary surface that you can easily trace your pattern onto and then needle-felt through.

Water-soluble stabiliser (such as Sulky's *Super Solvy Water Soluble Stabilizer*) is commonly used for embroidery and is available from most sewing or craft stores. You can trace or print your pattern onto this product, place it on top of your fabric, and needle-felt directly through it.

Fusible interfacing offers another option. You can trace your pattern onto the interfacing, then lightly fuse it to your fabric using an iron before needle-felting through it.

Water-soluble stabilisers and interfacings vary in thickness and behaviour, so it is important to test your chosen product first to ensure that you can needle-felt through it comfortably.

Some transfer papers are self-adhesive, while others will need to be pinned in place.

Before completing your piece, ensure that any exposed transfer paper is either fully covered with fibre or dissolved with water.

IRON-ON TRANSFER PEN

If you are working onto a fully opaque base (such as a wool felt sheet), you can transfer your pattern using an iron-on transfer method.

Trace your pattern onto standard paper (such as 80gsm photocopy paper) using an iron-on transfer pen – you can use the light pad or window tracing method for this.

Place the paper face down onto your base material, then press with a dry iron (no steam) to transfer the image.

Important: The image must be traced in ***reverse****, as it will flip during the transfer process. For this reason, all patterns in this book are provided both right way round and reversed, so you can choose the method that works best for your materials.*

PINNING THE FABRIC

Pin the fabric with your transferred pattern onto the foam pad.

Position the pins around the perimeter, ensuring the fabric is taut but not overstretched. You will need 12–18 sewing pins to secure the fabric in place.

It is vital, when pinning your work for the first layer of the felting process, that the outer border is straight (both vertically and horizontally), with no kinks in the lines. This will ensure that your finished bookmark is also straight.

You will be removing and re-pinning the fabric in this same manner after each layer of your fibre painting.

NOTE: To achieve the fringe effect, you will need to pin your **two layers** together (as shown in the photo above). Lay your felt layer on the foam first, then place the fabric layer on top, and pin through both layers to secure them to the foam.

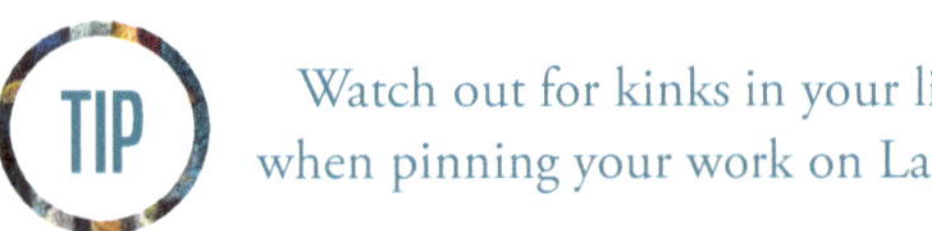

Watch out for kinks in your lines when pinning your work on Layer 1!

STARTING OUT

1. Select the wool fibre in the colour you want to use. Pull off a small piece of fibre (about the size of a coin) to start with. You can always add more wool as needed and you'll soon get the feel of how much wool to use for different-sized areas.

2. Pull the fibre apart repeatedly with your fingers to 'rough it up' a bit, which makes the fibre easier to needle-felt.

3. Hold your felting needle in your writing hand. Place the fibre on the section where you want it to go, and hold it in place lightly with your index finger. Begin by gently poking/needling the wool into the fabric base. Be careful to keep your fingers clear of the needle's path to avoid injury (it's handy to keep plasters close by). Use a straight up-and-down motion (as close to a 90° angle to the fabric as possible), needling the fibre repeatedly.

   The more you needle the fibre into the fabric, the denser and firmer the fibres will become. To replicate the style of needle-felting in this book, you will need to needle the fibres a lot to flatten the wool to the surface of the fabric. Keep your fibres somewhat loose on Layer 1, as you have Layers 2, 3 and 4 to fully-flatten the fibre.

4. Start by needling around the outline of a section, then gently fold the fibre ends into the centre of the section to define the shape you want, needling the fibre as you go. **You should not be able to see any of the fabric base between the sections.**

5. To add more wool, pull off small pieces and place them onto your artwork. Felt them in by needling them until they adhere. You will be building up layers to create depth and texture, highlights and shadows, colour blends and details.

6 You can mix fibre colours by hand to create custom shades and gradients. Select small amounts of each colour you wish to blend. Lay the fibres on top of each other and gently pull them apart, then stack the pulled sections back together. Repeat this process several times, pulling and stacking, until the fibres are thoroughly mixed and you achieve the desired blend. This method ensures a smooth and even colour transition, giving you greater control over the hues in your felted artwork. You can use two small carding brushes to achieve a stronger blend (two wire-bristle dog brushes will give a similar result).

7 Once you're satisfied with the overall look, give the entire piece one final needling pass to ensure everything is secure and smooth. Poke any loose fibres in with your needle. Use scissors only if absolutely necessary, as they create a blunt edge on the fibre which can be difficult to felt into your artwork.

TIPS FOR SUCCESS:

- Be patient and take your time – felting is a slow process.
- Start by felting simple shapes to build your skills and confidence.
- Try using different gauge needles until you find the needle size that works well for you.
- Try using different needle handles to find the most comfortable one for you.
- Needle in all the wispy fibre ends as you go, to keep your work neat and prevent the colours from blending unintentionally.
- It is better to use small quantities of fibre and work up in layers. The thicker the fibre, the higher the chance of your needle breaking.
- When blending fibres, save any surplus for later. Reusing the same blends keeps your colour palette consistent and reduces fibre waste.

Check out the Troubleshooting section (page 26) if things aren't quite turning out as you hoped!

Creating art often requires patience, perseverance, and trust, particularly when the process involves phases that feel far removed from the final vision.

In my needle-felting journey, I've learned that to create something truly beautiful, I must first navigate through the stages of "boring" and "ugly" before arriving at "beautiful." Each stage is vital, even though the first two can be challenging to endure and even harder to embrace.

For the majority of these projects (particularly during Layers 1, 2, and 3) you may find yourself wondering if it will ever start to look good!

LAYER 1: THE "BORING" STAGE

The first layer is all about building a foundation. It's necessary, but admittedly uninspiring. The work at this stage often looks flat and lacks the depth that will eventually emerge. Filling in all the sections can feel like a monotonous task, but it's a crucial step in the process.

LAYER 2: THE "UGLY" STAGE

Next comes the "ugly" stage. This is where you add the emphasis lines that will eventually create shadows and depth. At this point, your work might appear rough, unfinished, cartoonish and far from beautiful. Doubts may creep in, and you might even feel tempted to give up or start over. But this stage is pivotal for the transformation ahead.

LAYER 3: THE UPHILL JOURNEY

This layer involves refining and enhancing details and blends, bringing you closer to the final result.

LAYER 4: THE "BEAUTIFUL" STAGE

At last, all your hard work pays off. In Layer 4, the vision you've held onto will shine. The depth, texture, highlights and details emerge, transforming what once felt uncertain into something remarkable.

Remember to trust the process – it works!

TEST SQUARES

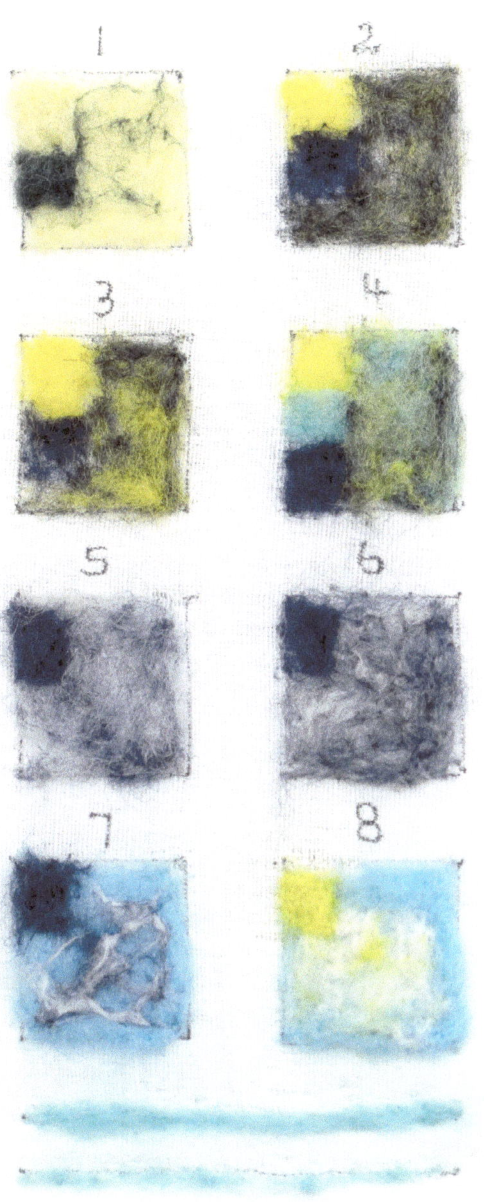

When you first start needle-felting and experimenting with colour blending, the process can feel a bit overwhelming. A great way to build confidence before diving into your fibre painting is to create a series of test squares (or patches).

On a spare piece of fabric (or within the outer perimeter of your artwork) use a black permanent marker or ballpoint pen to draw eight small squares and two lines.

SQUARES: Number the squares 1 to 8 so you can remember how you created each effect. Then, using the needle-felting process (see page 15) and your wool and cotton fibres, experiment by felting each square as follows:

1 Using **wool** fibre, felt the square with one colour. Then add a wisp of another colour (a fine layer) over the top so that you see some of the base colour showing through. You do not have to cover the whole of the base layer – this is one way of creating a blend.

2 Select two colours of **wool** fibre (be mindful of colour theory). Blend them together a lot until it looks like a new colour, and felt the square.

3 Select two colours of **wool** fibre. Blend them together just a little bit (so you can see each colour distinctly) and felt the square. Notice the strong gradation of colour.

4 Select three different colours of **wool** fibre (be mindful of colour theory) and blend them together, then felt the square.

5 Blend **white wool** fibre with a **colour wool** fibre and felt the square.

6 Blend **white cotton** fibre with the **same colour wool** fibre used in #5 and felt the square.

7 Felt the square with any colour **wool** fibre(s). Blend **white cotton** fibre and a **coloured wool** fibre (around 70% cotton/30% wool). Add a small amount of this blend over the base colour, so that some of the base can be seen.

8 Felt the square with any colour **wool** fibre(s). Blend **white cotton** fibre with **white wool** fibre (around 70% cotton/30% wool). Add a small amount of this blend over the base colour. Then take any colour wool fibre and add a tiny wisp of colour over the white cotton blend to create a brighter version of the colour. See how the colour glows!

You can create similar test squares to try out new types of fibres, different breeds of wool, different colours, colour theory experiments, etc.

LINES: Following the instructions on page 21, '*How to create a line*', make your first line a thick line, and make your second line a thin line. Keep the thickness of your lines consistent across the whole length.

LAYER 1

Layer 1 forms the foundation of your fibre painting. This is where you'll lay down the base colours and begin to bring your pattern to life.

While the process may feel slow at first, it's important to focus on building a solid base with thoughtful colour choices and careful blending.

This layer is not about perfection but rather setting the stage for the depth and detail that will come in later layers.

Here are instructions and tips to help you work through Layer 1 effectively:

- Needle-felt the sections of the pattern, either matching the colours to the original as closely as you can, or creating a colour palette your own unique way.
- You can start anywhere and felt the sections in whatever order you wish.
- Take a very small amount of fibre, pull it apart repeatedly with your fingertips to fluff it up, then begin filling in each section of the pattern.
- Roughly outline a section by needling the fibre along the pattern lines. Then, gently fold the fibre back into the section and needle-felt the ends to tidy them up. Felt right up to the black lines (there should be no white fabric showing in between the sections).
- If you have too much fibre in a section, hold your work down with one finger and use your other hand to pull away the excess. Then felt in the leftover wisps. You should never need to cut your fibre with scissors using this method. It's better to work in thin layers rather than trying to felt too much fibre at once.
- Black is a dominant colour and can consume other colours quickly, so use black wisely and sparingly. Consider mixing black with other colours to create shades (see the Colour Theory section page 11).
- Pattern sections are rarely solid blocks of colour. Each section should display a mix of colours. Layer 1 is an excellent time to experiment with your colour blends. If you don't like the result, you can gently try to remove some of the fibre, or simply felt over your work.
- If you are layering colours to create a blend from dark to light, then lay down your dark colour first, then mid, then light.
- Each fibre painting project is created in four layers. While you can lay blocks of solid colours on Layer 1 and build up additional colours in Layers 3 and 4, you'll achieve a richer result if you start blending your colours from Layer 1.
- Use very small amounts of two or three colours and mix them using your fingertips or two small carding brushes. The more you pull and mix the colours, the more seamlessly they will blend.
- Continue adding colour until you have covered the entire image.
- For a bookmark, it's important that the outer perimeter has clean edges. Felt in all wispy fibres.
- Avoid felting Layer 1 too flat. Felt just enough to secure the fibres and tuck in the wispy ends. Additional layers will be added, with flattening done in Layers 3 and 4.

To create tints (lighter colours) on Layers 1, 2, and 3, mix your colours with the white **wool** fibre. Save the white **cotton** fibre for the final highlights on Layer 4. This is because cotton is thick and opaque, making it ideal for creating bold highlights, while wool is more translucent and easier to needle-felt over.

REMOVE AND RE-PIN LAYER 1

To achieve a professional finish, it's important to regularly remove and re-pin your fabric while needle-felting.

If the fabric stays pinned to the foam for too long, pieces of foam can become entangled in the back of your artwork. These foam pieces can be difficult to remove and may prevent your finished artwork from lying completely flat. By removing and re-pinning the fabric **after each layer**, you'll avoid these issues and ensure a smooth, clean result.

1. Remove all the pins.
2. Gently peel the fabric away from the foam base. Start at one corner or along one edge, carefully lifting the fabric, and then peel it back. Repeat this around all edges until the fabric is completely removed from the foam.
3. Re-pin the fabric to the foam base in the same way you did initially, ensuring it is taut but not overstretched.

LAYER 2

Layer 2 is where your artwork begins to take shape, adding depth and structure to your composition.

On this layer you will add "emphasis lines", which are wispy strands of fibre applied to create dark lines defining and separating the sections. These lines can vary from bold and dramatic to subtle and understated, depending on the look you wish to achieve.

Don't be discouraged if the lines appear stark or overly dark at this stage as, in Layer 3, you'll soften and blend them into the artwork.

HOW TO CREATE A LINE

Anchor the fibre at the start of your line by poking it into place with your needle. Keeping the needle in the fibre, gently pull the fibre to extend the strand into a long, thin line. Needle-felt the fibre into place, working along the length of the line.

Don't worry if the line breaks, just start felting the line again from where the break happened. You will be covering over these lines in Layer 3, so perfection is not required here!

WHAT TO FOCUS ON

- All patterns in this book use emphasis lines. However, as an alternative, you could leave Layer 2 out completely for a more subtle, blended appearance. I suggest trying one pattern with all four layers to start with, so that you understand my process and the results you can achieve.
- Most sections (but not necessarily all) will have emphasis lines in them. I sometimes leave out the lines in background areas such as the sky in 'Up' (page 36).
- Start fine. Begin with thin lines. If you want them darker or thicker, add more fibre gradually. Some lines will remain thin, while others can be thicker, depending on your preference. Don't make your lines too thick or your painting could end up looking like a stained glass picture.
- Try to avoid using solid black for the lines. Instead, use dark shades of other colours. If the fibre you have is not dark enough, blend your chosen colour with a small amount of black to create the desired shade.
- To determine what colour line to use, look at the design. If the design element you are outlining is leaves, then use dark green. If it's sky, use dark blue. If it's land, then use dark brown, If it's rose petals, use a dark burgundy, etc. If the line is in between two different elements (e.g. sky and trees), then choose a colour to match the foreground element (e.g. the trees).

Remember to remove the fabric from the foam and re-pin before you begin Layer 3!

LAYER 3

Layer 3 is where you start to see what the artwork will look like when finished. This layer softens the emphasis lines from Layer 2, enhances colour transitions, and adds depth to your piece. It's also a chance to make adjustments to the colour and blending.

The key to Layer 3 is subtlety – less is more. By working with small amounts of fibre and building up gradually, you can create smooth transitions while letting the colours from earlier layers shine through.

WHAT TO FOCUS ON

- Cover emphasis lines. Start by selecting a **wispy** amount of wool fibre that matches the section adjacent to each emphasis line. The goal is to partially or fully cover the lines you created in Layer 2 (to soften the lines and blend them slightly with the adjacent section) while allowing some of the dark colour underneath to remain visible.
- Enhance or correct blending. If you want to enhance or change areas, now is the time. Use minimal fibre so that the colours from Layer 1 still show through, creating depth and vibrancy. Aim for smooth blends instead of hard lines.
- Work in light layers. Build up colour using multiple thin layers of wispy fibre rather than a single heavy application. This method gives you more control and avoids overpowering the earlier layers.
- Balance coverage. In some sections you may decide to cover Layer 1 completely to refine or change your design. Or, you may choose to let the original colours peek through for a rich, layered effect.
- Redefine the sections. Use Layer 3 to crisply felt the edges of your sections or change the shape of a section completely!
- Layer 1 choices impact Layer 3. If you blended colours on Layer 1, you'll need less blending work on Layer 3. If you used solid blocks of colour on Layer 1, focus on creating smooth colour transitions during Layer 3.
- Use colour theory. Try using complementary and analogous colour combinations to ensure harmonious blends that enhance the overall composition.

It's time to remove and re-pin!

Coloured wool fibre lightly mixed with white cotton fibre.

LAYER 4

We're nearly there! Layer 4 is where you finish your fibre painting by adding highlights, shadows, and fine details. It's your last opportunity to correct colours, tidy blends, and ensure your bookmark is finished.

Highlights and shadows are key to this layer, helping to emphasise depth and dimension. Now is the time to use **white cotton** fibre to add bright, opaque highlights.

WHAT TO FOCUS ON

- Add highlights and shadows:
  For white highlights, blend **white cotton** fibre (70%) and **white wool** fibre (30%). Cotton fibres are smooth, so you need to mix them with wool's scaly fibres for felting to work.
  For coloured highlights (*see picture above*), blend **white cotton** fibre (70%) with **coloured wool** fibre (30%). Adjust the lightness by increasing or decreasing the coloured fibre. Experiment with highlight colours to add character.
- Apply highlights to most sections, and consider adding fine wisps of colour wool fibre over the cotton fibre for a unique effect.
- Define with outlines. You can use the dark colour mixes from Layer 2 to create **very fine** outlines around **some** sections, adding subtle definition without overpowering the piece. Try it on a couple of sections to see if outlining is appropriate. As an alternative, you can try outlining some of your sections with a complementary colour. For example, if you have a green section, try outlining with a tiny wisp of red along the border.
- Evaluate and adjust. Stand back and assess your felting objectively (squinting your eyes can help):

  Check the tonality–are any areas too light or too dark?
  Do you need to add more highlights or shadows?
  Are blends smooth enough?
  Are the colours balanced?
- Finish with care. Needle over the entire image to secure loose ends and make it as flat as possible.
- Ensure no white fabric or pen lines are visible between the sections. Cover these areas with a small amount of fibre if needed.

Layer 4 can be tough on your needle due to the thicker fibre layers, especially where cotton is used. Keep your needle upright and work gently to avoid breakages.

EXAMPLES OF HIGHLIGHTS

EXAMPLES OF SHADOWS

KNOWING WHEN TO STOP

How do you know when to stop felting and say "*it's done*"?

When I left school, I began an apprenticeship in photolithography, a part of the printing trade that essentially served the same purpose as graphic design does today – before computers transformed the industry. This was back in the early 90s, and our Foreman, Ted Sherwen, was not only my supervisor but also a prolific and highly respected watercolour painter in New Zealand.

Ted taught night school watercolour classes. Since there was no digital photography back then, he would document every step of his process using 35mm slides. He'd bring these slides into work and, knowing I had an interest in art, he'd lay them out in sequence on the large light tables in our studio. With his thick Scottish accent, he would point to each slide in turn and say, "*Sarah, you listen to me: $100, $200, $300, $400... $300, $200, $100. You need to know when to stop.*"

That lesson has stuck with me ever since. There's a moment in every artwork where continuing to add more might not improve it but risk overworking it. Sometimes simplicity is the key, and other times complexity works better – it depends on your style and vision. But knowing when to step back and say, "*it's done*" is a skill every artist must develop.

Take a moment to reflect on your own work. Are you at risk of doing one needle poke too many, of adding that final touch that detracts rather than enhances? Recognising that tipping point can be the difference between a piece that feels fresh and intentional, and one that feels overworked. It's a skill worth practising.

IRONING YOUR WORK

You've finished, well done! Remove all the pins and carefully peel your artwork off the foam block.

As you've been removing and re-pinning your fabric after each layer, there should (hopefully) be no foam pieces embedded in the back of your artwork. If there are any, try picking them out with your fingers, or use a carding brush (with metal teeth) to gently pull the foam away. Be as careful as possible to avoid damaging the front of your work.

If pieces of your foam block have come away, you can use the other side for your next needle-felting project. It's normal for foam to wear down over time after multiple uses.

Use a hot iron (**on the steam setting**) directly on the front of your work to smooth out the needle holes. You'll notice the fibres blending in a new way, and your artwork will take on a soft, buttery texture with rich, vibrant colours.

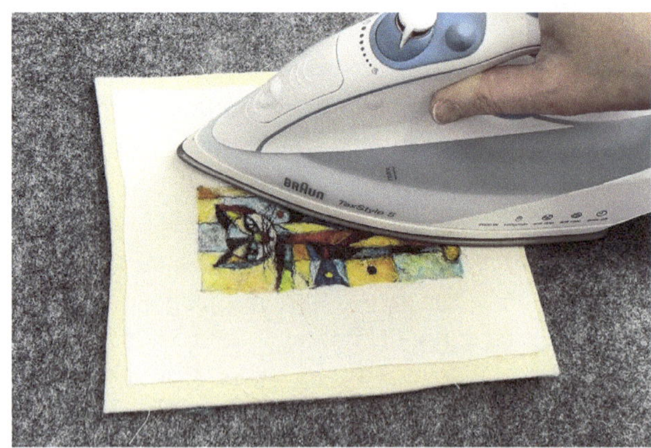

FINISHING YOUR BOOKMARK

There are many ways to finish the edges of your bookmark, depending on the look you would like to achieve. Here are a few ideas:

- **CROCHET EDGING:** A crochet edge adds a soft, decorative border. You can work directly into the felt or fabric using a fine hook, creating anything from a simple stitch to a more intricate lace-like finish.
- **HAND STITCHING:** A simple blanket stitch or decorative hand stitch can frame your bookmark beautifully.
- **SEWING MACHINE EDGING:** Using a sewing machine is a quick and effective way to create a clean, durable edge. Try zig-zag stitch, overlocking stitch, embroidery stitches or even a simple straight stitch around the edge (just inside the border).
- **FABRIC BACKING AND TURNED EDGE:** You can attach a backing fabric, sew around the edges, turn the bookmark through and press to create a clean, enclosed edge. This gives a more polished, fabric-based finish.
- **LEFT RAW (FELT ONLY):** If you are working directly onto wool felt, leaving the edge raw (cut with standard or pinking scissors) can be a beautiful and intentional choice. The felt will not fray.

Choose the finish that best suits your design and materials – there is no single "right" way, only the one that works for you.

CREATING THE FRINGE EFFECT

1

Carefully hold back the top fabric layer. Cut the wool felt layer close to your felting work, taking care not to cut into the design, as you may also catch the top fabric layer. Trim away all excess wool felt.

2

Trim the top fabric layer all the way around your bookmark. The width of fabric you leave will become the length of your fringe. You can always trim the fringe later if it is too long.

3

To create the fringe, carefully and patiently remove the rows of threads from around the bookmark. Gently pull the threads away until they are all removed, leaving a soft, even fringe.

TROUBLESHOOTING

If the fibre isn't sticking to the fabric base.	Ensure you are applying enough downward pressure on the needle. Try changing needles as the needle you are using may be faulty or poor quality. If you work with cheap or inappropriate needles, it can feel like the needle is sliding through the fibre without catching. You should be able to feel the wool fibre becoming firm within a few pokes of the needle.
If the needle breaks.	Avoid using too much force and always insert the needle straight in and pull it straight out. Needles are fragile and can break if twisted or bent or used on an angle. A needle can also break if you try to push it through a very thick or knotty area of fibre.
If the wool looks uneven.	Keep your felting strokes consistent and work in small sections. Adding thin layers of wool gradually can help achieve a smoother finish.
If the colours are mixing unintentionally.	Work slowly and carefully when adding new colours. Be intentional with the colours you add – following colour theory will help to control your colour blends. Felt in wispy ends as you go.
If the needle gets stuck.	Gently wiggle the needle to free it, then check for any tangles or knots in the wool. Avoid pulling too hard, or pulling on an angle, to prevent breaking the needle.
If you make a mistake.	You can either try removing the section of fibre you have just felted, or felt over the section with another colour fibre.
If the fibre balls into a dense, small area when you start felting.	You are most likely placing fibre on your material then letting the fibre go before felting. You need to hold the fibre in place as you felt. Use the index finger of your non-felting hand to lightly hold the fibre.
If the fabric rips when removing it from the foam.	This can sometimes happen when you repeatedly poke the needle in the same place, weakening the base fabric. Firstly, do not panic – your work is still salvageable! Buy an iron-on fabric patch or iron-on interfacing from a sewing supplies store. Choose a patch colour that most closely matches the colour in the area that has ripped (just in case a bit of the patch shows through. Iron the patch to the **reverse** side of your artwork, where the rip is. You may also need to glue some fibres into place on the front. If you use glue make sure it is craft glue that is designed for fabric, and one that dries clear.

REPRODUCING THE PATTERNS

You'll need to photocopy (or scan and print) your chosen pattern from this book so that you can easily transfer it to your fabric base (see page 13).

Each bookmark pattern on the following pages is designed to be 55mm wide × 140mm high when reproduced at 100% (actual) size. However, you can enlarge the pattern if you wish. I recommend not reducing the size, as some of the design elements may become difficult to work at a smaller scale.

USING THE IRON-ON TRANSFER METHOD

Each pattern has been supplied as both the **original design** (right way round) and the **reverse**.

If you are tracing the pattern onto a light-coloured fabric (using a light box, light pad, or window), you will use the original design.

If you are using an iron-on transfer pen or heat transfer sheet, you will need to use the reverse pattern. This is because when you place your paper (with the transfer image on it) onto your fabric base, the image will transfer in reverse.

WHICH PATTERN SHOULD I USE?

Use the original pattern (right way round) if:

- Your fabric is light in colour.
- Your fabric is slightly transparent.
- You are using a light pad, light box, or window to trace.
- You are using water-soluble transfer paper.
- You are using fusible interfacing.

Use the reverse pattern if:

- You are using an iron-on transfer pen.
- You are using another heat transfer method (such as printed heat transfer sheets).

If in doubt, think about how the image is being transferred – **if it flips during the process, you'll need the reverse pattern.**

CHIRP

LAYER 1

The most fiddly part of *Chirp* is the little white dot in the centre of Chirp's eye. Do this last. Use a tiny amount of white cotton fibre (or white wool fibre). Just a couple of pokes of the felting needle should do it!

LAYER 2

LAYER 3

LAYER 4 – FINISHED

CHIRP PATTERN

ORIGINAL DESIGN

'CHIRP' | ORIGINAL DESIGN BY SARAH RITCHIE ©2026. ALL RIGHTS RESERVED.

This pattern is protected by copyright law. Reproduction, distribution, or sale of this pattern or any part thereof is prohibited without the express written permission of the copyright holder. This pattern is intended for personal use only. Commercial use of the finished product is not allowed.

For permissions, please contact Sarah Ritchie via the website contact form at sarah-ritchie.com

REVERSE

'CHIRP' | ORIGINAL DESIGN BY SARAH RITCHIE ©2026. ALL RIGHTS RESERVED.

This pattern is protected by copyright law. Reproduction, distribution, or sale of this pattern or any part thereof is prohibited without the express written permission of the copyright holder. This pattern is intended for personal use only. Commercial use of the finished product is not allowed.
For permissions, please contact Sarah Ritchie via the website contact form at sarah-ritchie.com

SANDS

LAYER 1

The sky area of *Sands* is where you have freedom to play. You could make the sky one single colour, or a gradation of colour, or you could add in wispy clouds. Just remember to avoid using the white cotton fibre until the final layer.

LAYER 2

LAYER 3

LAYER 4 – FINISHED

SANDS PATTERN

ORIGINAL DESIGN

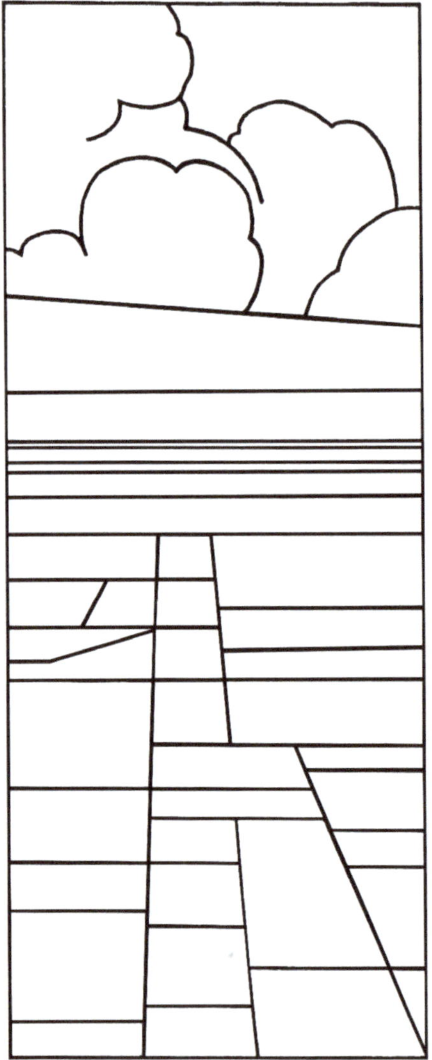

'SANDS' | ORIGINAL DESIGN BY SARAH RITCHIE ©2026. ALL RIGHTS RESERVED.

This pattern is protected by copyright law. Reproduction, distribution, or sale of this pattern or any part thereof is prohibited without the express written permission of the copyright holder. This pattern is intended for personal use only. Commercial use of the finished product is not allowed.

For permissions, please contact Sarah Ritchie via the website contact form at sarah-ritchie.com

REVERSE

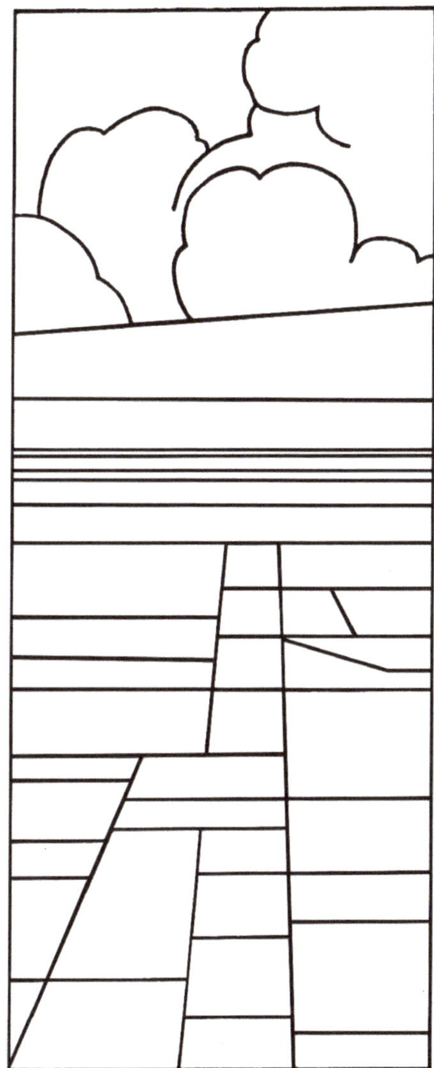

'SANDS' | ORIGINAL DESIGN BY SARAH RITCHIE ©2026. ALL RIGHTS RESERVED.

This pattern is protected by copyright law. Reproduction, distribution, or sale of this pattern or any part thereof is prohibited without the express written permission of the copyright holder. This pattern is intended for personal use only. Commercial use of the finished product is not allowed.
For permissions, please contact Sarah Ritchie via the website contact form at sarah-ritchie.com

UP

LAYER 1

Up is a simple project to complete with no tricky sections. To keep the sky looking fluffy and separate from the balloon, you may choose not to include any emphasis lines at all (as in the example, below).

LAYER 2

LAYER 3

LAYER 4 – FINISHED

UP PATTERN

ORIGINAL DESIGN

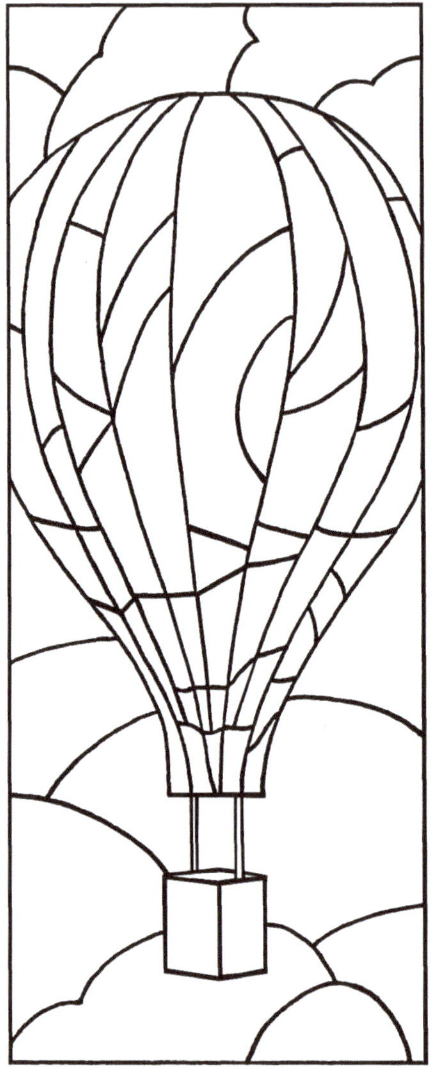

'UP' | ORIGINAL DESIGN BY SARAH RITCHIE ©2026. ALL RIGHTS RESERVED.

This pattern is protected by copyright law. Reproduction, distribution, or sale of this pattern or any part thereof is prohibited without the express written permission of the copyright holder. This pattern is intended for personal use only. Commercial use of the finished product is not allowed.
For permissions, please contact Sarah Ritchie via the website contact form at sarah-ritchie.com

REVERSE

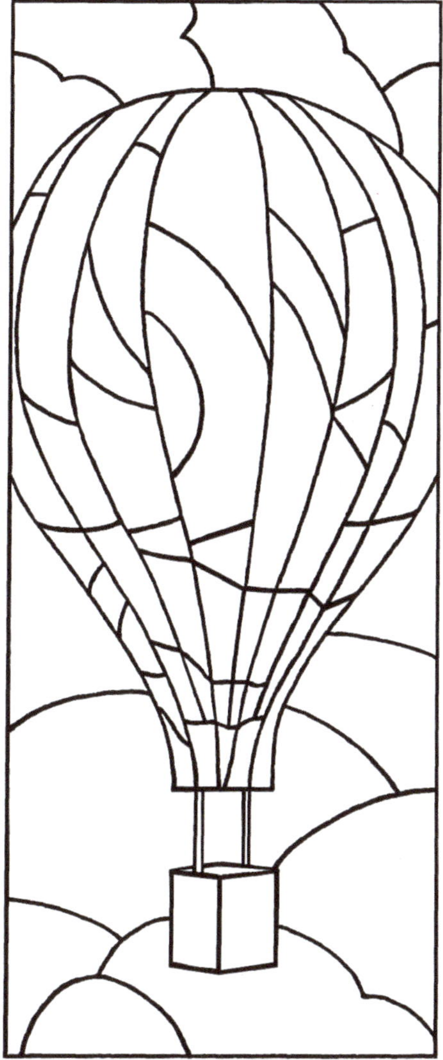

'UP' | ORIGINAL DESIGN BY SARAH RITCHIE ©2026. ALL RIGHTS RESERVED.

This pattern is protected by copyright law. Reproduction, distribution, or sale of this pattern or any part thereof is prohibited without the express written permission of the copyright holder. This pattern is intended for personal use only. Commercial use of the finished product is not allowed.
For permissions, please contact Sarah Ritchie via the website contact form at sarah-ritchie.com

FLEUR

LAYER 1

The trickiest parts of *Fleur* are the petals around the centre of the flower, as these segments are quite small. Use wisps of fibre in these areas to build the colour and blend gently.

LAYER 2

LAYER 3

LAYER 4 – FINISHED

FLEUR PATTERN

ORIGINAL DESIGN

'FLEUR' | ORIGINAL DESIGN BY SARAH RITCHIE ©2026. ALL RIGHTS RESERVED.

This pattern is protected by copyright law. Reproduction, distribution, or sale of this pattern or any part thereof is prohibited without the express written permission of the copyright holder. This pattern is intended for personal use only. Commercial use of the finished product is not allowed.

For permissions, please contact Sarah Ritchie via the website contact form at sarah-ritchie.com

REVERSE

'FLEUR' | ORIGINAL DESIGN BY SARAH RITCHIE ©2026. ALL RIGHTS RESERVED.

This pattern is protected by copyright law. Reproduction, distribution, or sale of this pattern or any part thereof is prohibited without the express written permission of the copyright holder. This pattern is intended for personal use only. Commercial use of the finished product is not allowed.
For permissions, please contact Sarah Ritchie via the website contact form at sarah-ritchie.com

BUDDY

LAYER 1

The eye of *Buddy* deserves the most attention in this design. On Layer 1, add the black area along with an orange circle. On Layer 3, add another black circle over the top of the orange. Then add a fine blue line to define the eye. Wait until Layer 4 to add the white highlight, using just a couple of stabs of white cotton fibre.

LAYER 2

LAYER 3

LAYER 4 – FINISHED

BUDDY PATTERN

ORIGINAL DESIGN

'BUDDY' | ORIGINAL DESIGN BY SARAH RITCHIE ©2026. ALL RIGHTS RESERVED.

This pattern is protected by copyright law. Reproduction, distribution, or sale of this pattern or any part thereof is prohibited without the express written permission of the copyright holder. This pattern is intended for personal use only. Commercial use of the finished product is not allowed. For permissions, please contact Sarah Ritchie via the website contact form at sarah-ritchie.com

REVERSE

'BUDDY' | ORIGINAL DESIGN BY SARAH RITCHIE ©2026. ALL RIGHTS RESERVED.

This pattern is protected by copyright law. Reproduction, distribution, or sale of this pattern or any part thereof is prohibited without the express written permission of the copyright holder. This pattern is intended for personal use only. Commercial use of the finished product is not allowed.

For permissions, please contact Sarah Ritchie via the website contact form at sarah-ritchie.com

ROAM

LAYER 1

There are no tricky areas in *Roam*. Simply fill in the segments, then finish the design with a few trees dotted here and there. The trees can be created as a series of small triangles.

LAYER 2

LAYER 3

LAYER 4 – FINISHED

ROAM PATTERN

ORIGINAL DESIGN

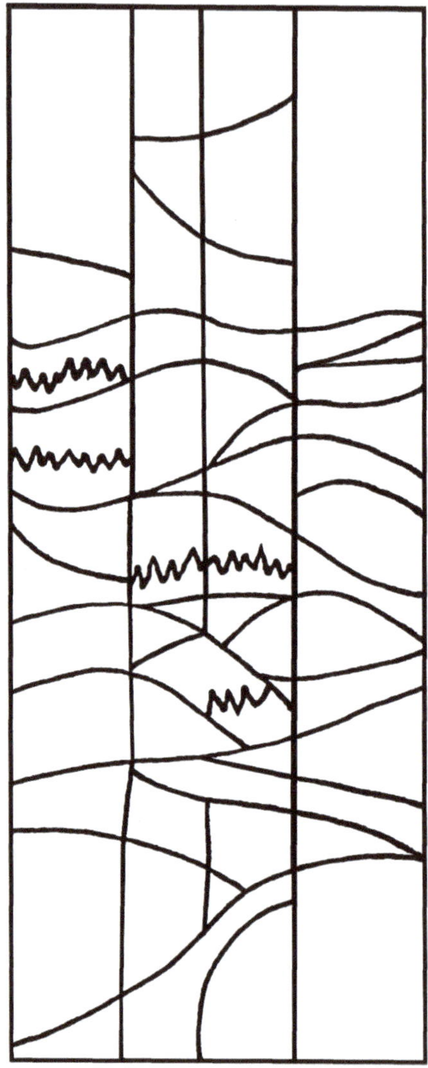

'ROAM' | ORIGINAL DESIGN BY SARAH RITCHIE ©2026. ALL RIGHTS RESERVED.

This pattern is protected by copyright law. Reproduction, distribution, or sale of this pattern or any part thereof is prohibited without the express written permission of the copyright holder. This pattern is intended for personal use only. Commercial use of the finished product is not allowed. For permissions, please contact Sarah Ritchie via the website contact form at sarah-ritchie.com

REVERSE

'ROAM' | ORIGINAL DESIGN BY SARAH RITCHIE ©2026. ALL RIGHTS RESERVED.

This pattern is protected by copyright law. Reproduction, distribution, or sale of this pattern or any part thereof is prohibited without the express written permission of the copyright holder. This pattern is intended for personal use only. Commercial use of the finished product is not allowed.
For permissions, please contact Sarah Ritchie via the website contact form at sarah-ritchie.com

WOOLLY

LAYER 1

Pay extra attention to *Woolly's* eyes and ears, as these are the fiddly parts of the design. Use small wisps of fibre and a light touch when felting. Use white cotton fibre to create the highlights, including the top of the head, ears, and eyes.

LAYER 2

LAYER 3

LAYER 4 – FINISHED

WOOLLY PATTERN

ORIGINAL DESIGN

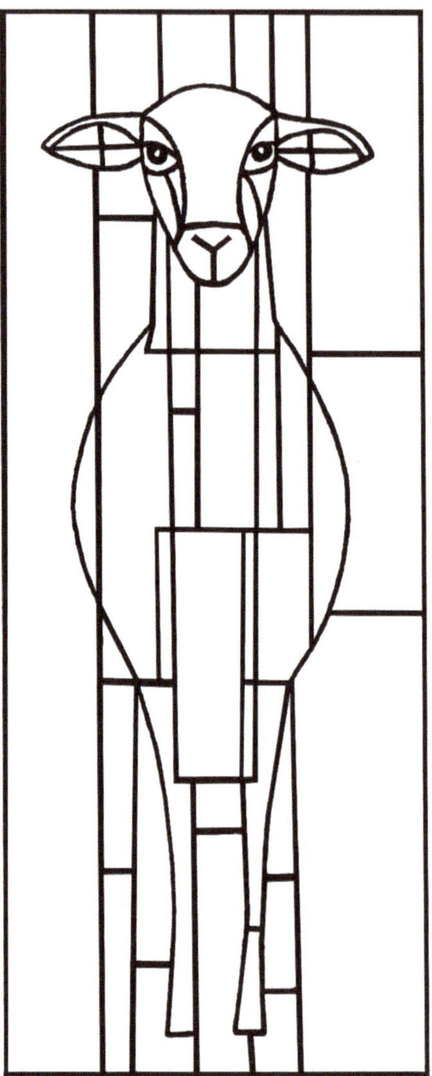

'WOOLLY' | ORIGINAL DESIGN BY SARAH RITCHIE ©2026. ALL RIGHTS RESERVED.

This pattern is protected by copyright law. Reproduction, distribution, or sale of this pattern or any part thereof is prohibited without the express written permission of the copyright holder. This pattern is intended for personal use only. Commercial use of the finished product is not allowed. For permissions, please contact Sarah Ritchie via the website contact form at sarah-ritchie.com

REVERSE

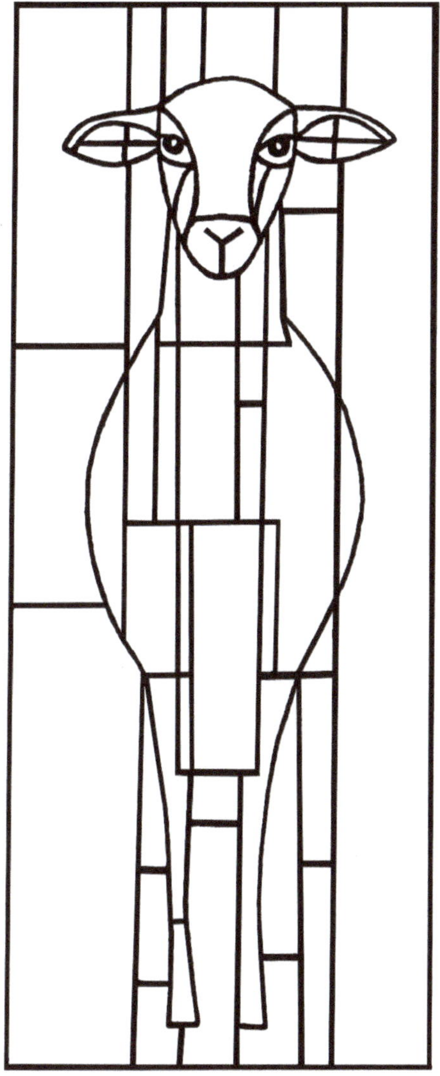

'WOOLLY' | ORIGINAL DESIGN BY SARAH RITCHIE ©2026. ALL RIGHTS RESERVED.

This pattern is protected by copyright law. Reproduction, distribution, or sale of this pattern or any part thereof is prohibited without the express written permission of the copyright holder. This pattern is intended for personal use only. Commercial use of the finished product is not allowed.
For permissions, please contact Sarah Ritchie via the website contact form at sarah-ritchie.com

WHISKER

LAYER 1

The trickiest parts of *Whisker* are around the eyes. Use very small amounts of fibre and a light touch when felting, and you'll be fine. Lastly, add fine, wispy lines for the whiskers and dots of white cotton fibre for the eye highlights.

LAYER 2

LAYER 3

LAYER 4 – FINISHED

WHISKER PATTERN

ORIGINAL DESIGN

'WHISKER' | ORIGINAL DESIGN BY SARAH RITCHIE ©2026. ALL RIGHTS RESERVED.

This pattern is protected by copyright law. Reproduction, distribution, or sale of this pattern or any part thereof is prohibited without the express written permission of the copyright holder. This pattern is intended for personal use only. Commercial use of the finished product is not allowed.

For permissions, please contact Sarah Ritchie via the website contact form at sarah-ritchie.com

REVERSE

'WHISKER' | ORIGINAL DESIGN BY SARAH RITCHIE ©2026. ALL RIGHTS RESERVED.

This pattern is protected by copyright law. Reproduction, distribution, or sale of this pattern or any part thereof is prohibited without the express written permission of the copyright holder. This pattern is intended for personal use only. Commercial use of the finished product is not allowed.

For permissions, please contact Sarah Ritchie via the website contact form at sarah-ritchie.com

INKY

LAYER 1

For *Inky*, you'll need to pay special attention to the long, thin legs and tentacles. The tentacles and mouth are added last.
The easiest way to create small dots is to take a small wisp of fibre, twirl it around the tip of the needle, then gently poke it into the fabric.

LAYER 2

LAYER 3

LAYER 4 – FINISHED

INKY PATTERN

ORIGINAL DESIGN

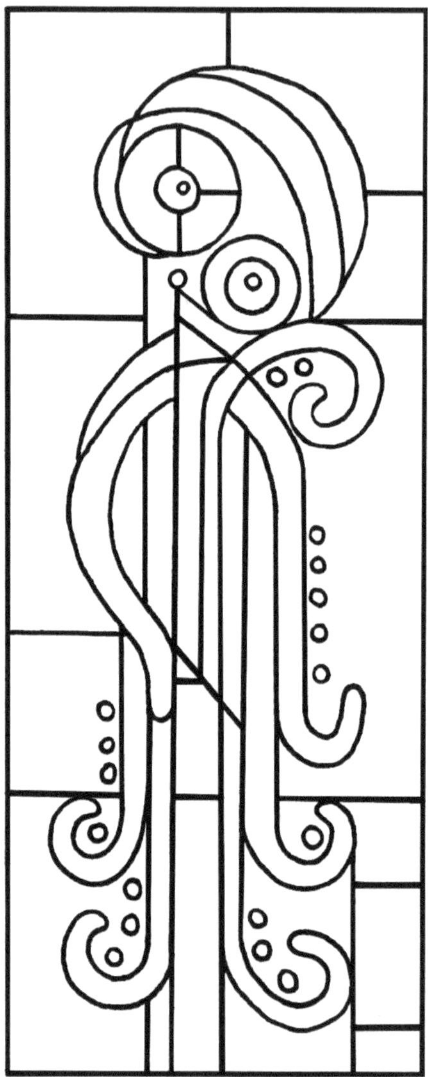

'INKY' | ORIGINAL DESIGN BY SARAH RITCHIE ©2026. ALL RIGHTS RESERVED.

This pattern is protected by copyright law. Reproduction, distribution, or sale of this pattern or any part thereof is prohibited without the express written permission of the copyright holder. This pattern is intended for personal use only. Commercial use of the finished product is not allowed.

For permissions, please contact Sarah Ritchie via the website contact form at sarah-ritchie.com

REVERSE

'INKY' | ORIGINAL DESIGN BY SARAH RITCHIE ©2026. ALL RIGHTS RESERVED.

This pattern is protected by copyright law. Reproduction, distribution, or sale of this pattern or any part thereof is prohibited without the express written permission of the copyright holder. This pattern is intended for personal use only. Commercial use of the finished product is not allowed.
For permissions, please contact Sarah Ritchie via the website contact form at sarah-ritchie.com

HARVEST

LAYER 1

Harvest is the most 'painterly' and three-dimensional of all the patterns in this book, which makes it the most challenging to complete. The light is coming from the left of the image, so all highlights will fall on the top left of the grapes, with shadows on the bottom right. For this design be ultra-mindful of your blends.

LAYER 2

LAYER 3

LAYER 4 – FINISHED

HARVEST PATTERN

ORIGINAL DESIGN

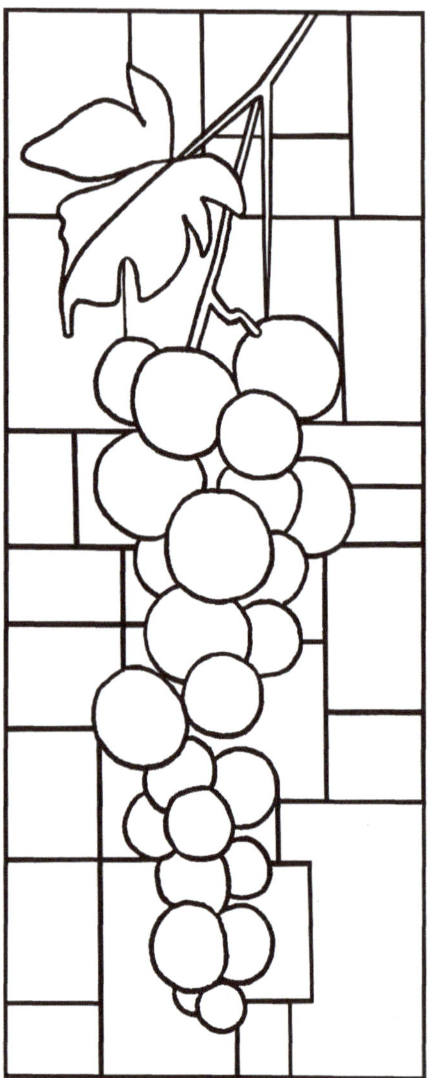

'HARVEST' | ORIGINAL DESIGN BY SARAH RITCHIE ©2026. ALL RIGHTS RESERVED.

This pattern is protected by copyright law. Reproduction, distribution, or sale of this pattern or any part thereof is prohibited without the express written permission of the copyright holder. This pattern is intended for personal use only. Commercial use of the finished product is not allowed.
For permissions, please contact Sarah Ritchie via the website contact form at sarah-ritchie.com

REVERSE

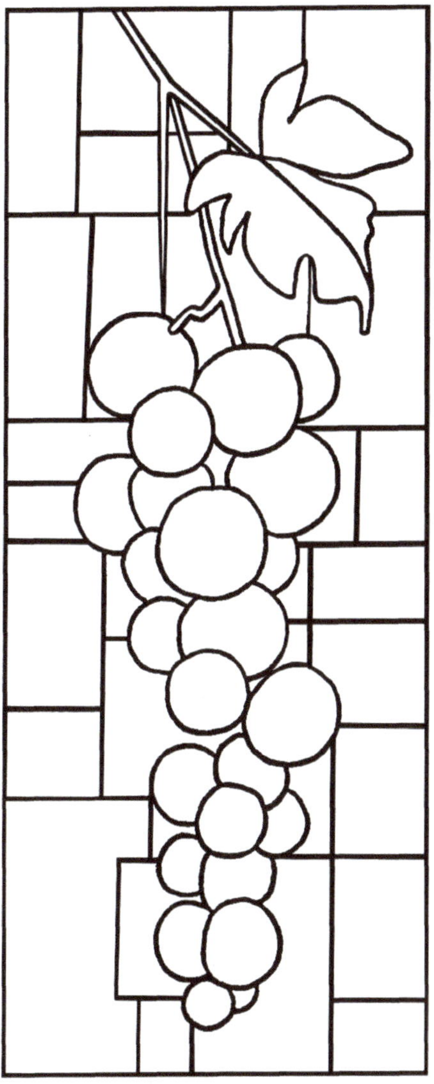

'HARVEST' | ORIGINAL DESIGN BY SARAH RITCHIE ©2026. ALL RIGHTS RESERVED.

This pattern is protected by copyright law. Reproduction, distribution, or sale of this pattern or any part thereof is prohibited without the express written permission of the copyright holder. This pattern is intended for personal use only. Commercial use of the finished product is not allowed. For permissions, please contact Sarah Ritchie via the website contact form at sarah-ritchie.com

WHERE WILL YOU GO NEXT?

As you reach the end of this book, I hope you've gained not only the skills to create your own needle-felted bookmarks but also the confidence to explore your creativity in new and exciting ways. Each project you've completed is a step forward on your creative journey, and where you go from here is entirely up to you.

Needle-felting is versatile and endlessly inspiring. From the small bookmarks you've created from this book to larger, more ambitious pieces, the possibilities are as limitless as your imagination. Whether you continue to refine your techniques, experiment with new styles, or even develop your own unique approach, needle-felting offers endless opportunities for artistic expression.

To spark your imagination, I've included a gallery of some of my larger fibre art pieces. These works represent what's possible when you blend artistry, patience, and passion with fibre painting. Let them inspire you to dream bigger and challenge yourself to take your skills to the next level.

Remember, every artist starts somewhere. What matters most is that you keep creating, keep experimenting, and keep pushing the boundaries of what's possible. Share your work with others, join communities of like-minded fibre artists, and don't be afraid to showcase your creations to the world.

Thank you for allowing me to guide you through this journey. I can't wait to see where your creativity takes you.

All the best,
Sarah Ritchie

All artworks shown are original needle-felted fibre paintings by Sarah Ritchie.

Opposite page:
'The Watchers Series: Hares Looking at You" (2025).

This page clockwise from top left:
'Ewetopia: Two Sheep in Aotearoa' (2023)
'City of Sails' (2023)
'Wild at Heart' (2026)
'Pīwakawaka' (2023)

Sarah Ritchie

ORIGINAL DESIGNS

BOOKS
KITS
ONLINE WORKSHOPS
PATTERNS

To keep up-to-date with Sarah's latest releases for kits, patterns, books, tutorials, workshops, artwork and more, visit sarah-ritchie.com and sign up to receive '*Musings*', Sarah's email newsletter.

Instagram: @sarahritchiehq
Facebook: facebook.com/sarahritchiehq

sarah-ritchie.com

MAKE SNAP SHARE

www.ingramcontent.com/pod-product-compliance
Lightning Source LLC
LaVergne TN
LVHW070143110826
845147LV00002B/319

* 9 7 8 0 4 7 3 7 8 5 5 3 6 *